Book of Saints For Catholic Children

By Rev. Daniel A. Lord, S.J.

NIHIL OBSTAT: Arthur J. Scanlan S. T. D., Censor Librorum
IMPRIMATUR: Francis J. Spellman, D. D., Archbishop, New York

Published by:
William J. Hirten Co.
Cumberland, Rhode Island

Saint Agatha

The Pure Virgin

Saint Agatha was very beautiful. People looked at her and said, "Oh, she is the fairest girl alive."

But Agatha was also very pure and good.

She loved Jesus Christ very much. She promised God she would never marry. "All my love is Yours," she said. "I will live and die for You."

Now it happened that the Governor of Sicily where Agatha lived heard of her beauty.

So he sent for her. Soldiers came and arrested her.

"You are a Christian," they said. "So you must go to jail." "Dear Lord Jesus," she prayed, "I belong to You. Do not let this tyrant have power over me."

He made love to her. But she refused him.

So he threw her into prison. The governor was sure Agatha would be so afraid of prison that she would consent to love him.

Instead, she made the wicked woman who was her jailer love God too.

So the Governor ordered her to be tortured. She was not afraid. Then he ordered her to be beaten.

"Dear Jesus," she cried, "come and take me."

And Jesus came and took her home to heaven.

Her Feast is February 5th.

Saint Agnes
Martyr

Agnes was only twelve when the Roman soldiers arrested her.

They were killing all Christians in those days. But first they dragged her to the statue of a false goddess.

Offer prayers and incense to Minerva," they ordered her. Instead, brave little Agnes lifted her arms and prayed aloud to Jesus Christ.

So they put handcuffs on her. She was so tiny that the cuffs slipped off her wrists.

Then they whipped her cruelly. They said they would stop if she gave up Jesus Christ. Even the pagans wept to see her tortured that way.

Next they dragged her through the streets for the people to laugh at. Instead, some of them tried to save her. Then a young man asked her to marry him.

"I will save you if you do," he promised.

I belong to my Savior alone," she answered.

With one stroke of the sword, the soldiers killed this brave little girl.

Her Feast is January 21st.

Saint Aloysius
Gonzaga

Aloysius was the son of a very famous and noble family.

They expected him to make a name for himself in the world.

Instead, he promised God he would never marry. He asked to love God and Our Lady alone.

When he was very young, he became a Jesuit. From the very start, he was as holy as he could be. He kept his soul as pure as the whitest snow.

He loved Mary with all his heart. He stayed for hours on his knees before Christ in the Blessed Sacrament.

But he was a brave young man. When a terrible sickness came over the city, Aloysius went out to care for the sick. Once he brought home a very sick old man and nursed him in his own bed.

He wanted very much to be a priest.

But God wanted to show young people that even the very young can be saints. So he took Aloysius early with him to Heaven.

He is the special patron of boys and girls. Boys and girls can all study as hard as he did. They can love Christ and Mary with all their hearts.

But most of all, they can be very pure.

His Feast is June 21st.

Saint Ambrose
Lawyer and Bishop

Ambrose was a successful lawyer and governor in Italy. When the Bishop of Milan died, the people began to fight about who would become the new Bishop.

As governor, Ambrose gave a great speech to bring peace back to the city. The people started shouting, "Ambrose for Bishop!" Ambrose was not even baptized at the time that the people wanted him to become Bishop.

So, he began studying Scripture and theology, gave all he had to the poor and was baptized and made Bishop on the same day. Ambrose became a great Bishop, always standing up for the poor people and always working for peace. One Palm Sunday, an army came to destroy the Cathedral in Milan. The troops surrounded the church trying to starve the people and make them come out but Ambrose and all the people stayed inside until Easter.

Ambrose made up songs about the goodness of God and the people sang so loud that the soldiers outside the Church could hear. Little by little, the soldiers turned their hearts to God and began singing along with the people inside the Cathedral. Everyone was allowed to go home in peace. Ambrose showed great courage as Bishop. He turned many people, including leaders of government to God. He is the patron of Bishops.

His Feast day is December 7th.

Saint Andrew

Apostle

Andrew was just a poor fisherman in Galilee. He had a brother whose name was Simon Peter.

One day he heard a great preacher, John the Baptist. He left his boats and fishing nets, and followed John.

And John said, "Someone is coming who is greater than I."

So when Jesus came, Andrew left John to follow Jesus. He ran and told Simon Peter. Peter went to Jesus too. Andrew and Peter both became Apostles.

Andrew was the Apostle who found the little boy with the loaves and fishes. Our dear Lord used these to feed thousands of people. That was a great miracle.

Jesus made Andrew one of His first Bishops.

"Go, teach everyone the Good News," Jesus said.

So after the Ascension of our Lord into heaven, Andrew went to Greece.

Some listened and became Christians.

But some hated Andrew because they hated Jesus.

So they nailed Andrew to a Cross. Andrew sang with joy because, like Jesus, he could die on the Cross.

He hung for two days on the Cross telling everyone about Jesus.

Then he went gloriously to heaven.

His Feast is November 30th.

Saint Angela
Friend of Girls

Angela de Merici was a lovely young Italian woman. She knew many poor girls.

Most of them did not know about Jesus Christ.

Many of them had never heard much about the lovely Mother of God.

Many of them were sinful and bad. But Angela knew this was because no one had taught them to be good.

So she gathered children around her and taught them about Jesus and Mary.

She helped sinful girls to become good once more.

She built houses where they could live and be safe from temptation.

She found fine, pure, wise young women to teach the children. She wanted sinless girls to help save sinful girls. She took Saint Ursula for her patron.

Then she invited good young women and pure, sweet girls to help her.

They became the first Ursuline Sisters.

They went all over the world teaching and helping little children and girls and young women.

Today there are thousands of these Sisters. They all call Saint Angela their Patroness and Holy Mother.

Her Feast is January 27th.

Saint Ann
Mother of the Blessed Virgin

Ann was a dear old lady who had been married a long time. But God had never sent her a child.

That made her sad.

She wanted a baby to brighten her home. She kept praying to God, and God heard her prayer.

Her lovely little baby was Mary.

But even her happy Mother did not know that this little girl would be the Mother of God.

Ann gave her daughter the best home she could.

She sent her to school in the Temple. She loved her very much.

All the time, God knew Ann would be the Grandmother of His Son.

Because she was so good to Mary, His Mother, Jesus made Ann a great saint.

When we pray to her, we know that Jesus, her Grandson, will listen to what she asks for us.

Her Feast is July 26th.

Saint Anthony
of Padua

When Anthony of Padua died, the children cried in the streets.

"Our dear father, Anthony is dead," they wept.

And all the bells of the churches rang of their own accord. Angels came to earth to ring the bells for the death of the saint.

Anthony wanted to be a martyr. He wanted to die for the love of Christ.

Instead, Our Lord asked him to work among the poor and needy.

So Anthony went about Italy working wonderful miracles for the people. He gave them miraculous food. He healed their sicknesses.

Whenever he spoke of Jesus, everyone listened and loved the Savior, too.

One night the Divine Child came to visit Anthony. He kissed the saint gently and told him how much He loved him. You have often seen statutes of Saint Anthony with the Child in his arms.

Ever since his death, he has done wonderful things for those who pray to him. He is still the Franciscan Miracle-worker.

His Feast is June 13th.

Saint Apollonia
Virgin

Apollonia was an older woman who never married but who spent her life teaching the goodness of God.

She lived in Egypt preaching the Word of God and being kind and caring to others. Even when she was old, she preached about God and risked her life to visit Christians in prison and to comfort them.

She cared about all of God's people and wanted them to love God and to be happy. She did not like the way the people of God were treated and she was not afraid to speak about her Faith.

One night, angry non-Christians began to riot in her city and attacked all who believed in the Faith.

She was captured and tortured and all her teeth were smashed with pinchers and knocked out. The angry mob gave her the choice of rejecting Jesus or of being burned to death but Apollonia would not go against her Faith. She died in the flames.

Many of the non-Christians turned to Christianity after watching her strength in the Faith and learning about her love for God and His people.

Because of the way she was tortured, she is known as the patron of dentists and of those who suffer from toothaches or other dental problems. Her Feast is February 9th.

Saint Augustine
Bishop and Doctor of the Church

When Augustine was a young man, he was very clever and bright. His mother, Monica, was a good Catholic. But Augustine couldn't be bothered.

He didn't want to believe what Christ taught. He knew that what Christ taught was the truth, but he did not want to be good. He led a very wicked life.

All this time, his mother, Monica, wept and prayed.

"Make my son a good man," she begged God. "Please make him believe and give up his sins."

One day Augustine heard that some of his friends had become Catholics. They were not nearly as bright as he was. "How silly and foolish I am," he thought.

"They will go to heaven. But I, to whom God gave such a fine mind, will lose my soul."

He ran to his mother and told her he wished to be good henceforth. She was very glad.

So he repented of his sins. He studied to be a priest.

He became a great Bishop. He did penance for his sins. And he wrote many wonderful books about God and the soul and goodness.

He fought untruth and he hated sin.

The young man who had been a sinner became the man who was a wise and holy saint.

His Feast is August 28th.

Saint Barbara
The Brave Martyr

When Barbara was a little girl, her wicked father imprisoned her in a high tower.

So Barbara lived in the tower with only the servants who cared for her. And she was very good.

One day a priest passed under her tower. He was singing about Jesus Christ. Barbara heard him. She asked him about his song. He told her all about the Savior. Barbara was overjoyed.

"I love Jesus too," she cried. "I am a Christian."

When her father heard this, he was furious.

In those days, it was against the law to love Jesus or to be a Christian. So this cruel father dragged his own daughter to the judge. "My daughter is a Christian," he cried. "She is not my daughter any longer."

"What shall we do with her?" the judge asked. For he saw that Barbara was good and pure.

"Do what the law orders," her father shouted. "Beat her until she is almost dead. Then chop off her head."

So the soldiers carried out that cruel order.

But suddenly they saw angels coming. The angels carried the soul of Barbara to heaven. And a terrible flash of lightning struck her cruel father and killed him where he stood.

Her traditional Feast is December 4th.

Saint Benedict
Father of Holy Monks

The name Benedict means Blessed.

When Benedict was a boy, he realized that he was living in sad, not blessed days.

The world was full of savage and evil men. They made war on everybody. They destroyed beautiful buildings and burned wise books. They thought it was amusing to be destructive. They were very cruel.

Even the schoolboys were wicked and mean. They laughed at Benedict because he tried to be good.

So he ran away from the evil men and the sinful boys. He hid himself in a mountain near Subiaco.

He prayed. He studied. He talked with God. He asked God to make cruel men gentle and wicked little boys pure. Soon many people heard about this wonderful young man. They hated war and evil men. So they ran up to the mountain and said to Benedict, "Let us stay with you." Benedict built beautiful houses which are called monasteries. He dressed the good men as monks.

His sister, Saint Scholastica, dressed the women as nuns or sisters. She built convents.

In these the men and women prayed. They studied. They loved peace. They asked God to forgive sinners.

These men and women were the first Benedictines.

His Feast is July 11th.

Saint Bernadette
of Lourdes

Bernadette's mother and father were very poor.

One day Bernadette went to gather firewood. She came to a cave near a flowing river. Her friends played and sang. But Bernadette stood still, her eyes wide with wonder. For she saw a beautiful Lady, who was dressed in blue and white. There were stars around the Lady's head. Roses were on her feet. Bernadette told her parents and friends. At first they did not believe her.

But Bernadette saw the lovely Lady again and again. The lovely Lady ordered her to dig. A fresh, cool spring came bubbling up out of the ground.

Sick people who bathed in it grew well. Many of the blind could see again.

"Build here," said the lovely Lady, "a great church. And tell people to pray and do penance and walk in processions."

They did all this. Soon the wonderful Shrine of Lourdes was built.

And Bernadette waited until after the Lady had made her last visit to her. Then she went into the convent. She became a nun.

All the world knows about Lourdes. It is a beautiful shrine of Our Lady.

Her traditional Feast is February 18th.

Saint Bernard
of Clairvaux

When Bernard went to be a monk and a priest, thirty of his young friends went with him.

Later on, his father became a priest. And all his brothers joined him in his monastery.

He had only one sister. At first she was very happy and vain. But soon she became a nun, too.

That all showed how people loved Bernard and followed him.

He built a great monastery in a valley called Clairvaux. It was so strict people said, "No one will join."

Instead, hundreds of brave young men came.

The Turks, who hated Christians, were very strong and had great armies.

Bernard taught soldiers how to be fine pure knights. They became the Knights of the Temple. He led the Christian armies to fight against the Turks.

He carried only a crucifix.

But most of all, he loved Christ and Our Lady.

As a boy, as a great priest, even in the army, he wrote beautiful songs to them.

Some of them we sing to this day.

His Feast is August 20th.

Saint Bonaventure
Cardinal - Bishop

Bonaventure was a great Franciscan Bishop. He was born in Italy and as a young man joined the order of St. Francis of Assisi. He went to Paris to study at the university and became good friends with St. Thomas Aquinas who had joined the order of St. Dominic.

The men in the same group with Bonaventure were fighting with one another because many of them wanted to follow the hard teachings of St. Francis and live alone and poor while others wanted to live in groups and study at the university and learn more about religion.

Bonaventure became the master general of the order and solved the problems. He found special places for the men to live together and to study so they could become better preachers and still live a simple life like St. Francis. Bonaventure was very smart and he taught that we can be holy by doing normal things in our lives really well and by constantly working at small things.

He taught about truth and peace and love, and wrote many books and letters teaching others more about the Church and Jesus. He also wrote a book about St. Francis of Assisi. He became a Cardinal-Bishop and after he died, the Church gave him the title "Doctor of the Church" which means that he wrote many books and papers that help us learn more about the Church.

His Feast Day is July 15th.

Saint Brigid

Generous Saint

Brigid was born near Kildare in Ireland and was baptized and inspired by St. Patrick at an early age.

She wanted to become a nun but her father did not want her to so she stayed at home and took care of those in need out of her father's house. She was very generous to the poor and gave them her father's milk, butter, flour and anything else they may have needed. One day she even gave a jeweled sword to a leper.

Her father knew then that it was time to grant her wish and let her become a nun.

Brigid founded a double monastery in Kildare which was made for both nuns and monks.

It became a center for religion and learning and helped to spread the faith throughout all of Ireland. Brigid was considered very holy and faithful and because of her work other monasteries were built.

Brigid once came upon an unholy man who was dying and in order to bring him to the Lord, she made a cross out of the rushes, like straw, that covered the ground. As she made the cross she told the man about Jesus and His death on the cross. Before the man died, he asked to be baptized.

Her Feast is February 1st.

Saint Camillus
The Minister to the Sick

When Camillus was a young man, he always seemed to be in trouble for fighting and gambling. After his mother died, he stayed with relatives who did not seem to care about him much and when he was old enough, he joined the army. His problems with fighting and gambling continued and after losing everything he owned, he went to work at a monastery.

He made a vow to change his bad habits and began studying at the monastery but an infected cut on his leg from when he was in the army kept him from being able to stay with the other monks. He went to St. Giacomo Hospital, where he had once been a patient and began to work there. He could see a great need for workers who cared more for the sick and the dying. He moved to Rome and with a few of his friends set up a house to care for the sick in Holy Ghost Hospital. He studied to be a priest and started his own order called the Ministers of the Sick. As more men joined the order, he started a new house that cared for people on ships who were dying and for troops out on the battlefields. The Ministers of the Sick helped to change the way sick people were treated. Camillus taught his ministers to treat even the sickest people with love. They had a red cross on their cape to remind them of the love of Jesus.

His Feast Day is July 14th.

Saint Catherine of Siena
The Dominican

Catherine of Siena was one of the greatest women that ever lived. When she was a little girl, our dear Lord appeared to her.

"Please give me your heart," He asked.

She gave it willingly. Jesus gave her His Sacred Heart in return. Many rich young men wanted to marry this beautiful girl. Instead, she became a Dominican Sister.

In those days, the Pope did not live in Rome. He had moved to France. Catherine went to see him.

"Holy Father," she said, "your place is in Rome. Come home to your people."

The Pope obeyed this simple little nun.

Many of the princes were furious. They did not want the Pope in Rome. So they tried to elect a false Pope.

Catherine, without fear, told them this was wrong. They were afraid of her. They listened and obeyed.

The Pope knew she was very wise, and often asked for her advice. She always told him just what Jesus wanted and what would please God.

Although she was only thirty-three when she died, the whole world knew this saintly girl. They loved this brave woman.

Her Feast is April 29th.

Saint Catherine
of Alexandria

Catherine was a very rich child, being the daughter of noble parents. She was able to go to school and studied very hard.

She was always very holy. During her studies she found time to pray quietly to God.

In the days of Catherine, the Christians were being persecuted.

When Catherine was 18 years old, she went to the Emperor, who was violently persecuting the Christians and told him that he must stop attacking the good people and also stop serving false gods.

The Emperor was insulted and put her in jail. He said that she must die by being tortured on a spiked wheel.

A miracle happened when she touched the wheel. It fell apart.

The Emperor then ordered her head to be cut off. When her head was cut off, the angels from heaven carried her body to Mount Sinai, where later a church and convent was built in her honor.

Her Feast is November 25th.

Saint Cecilia
Martyr

Cecilia was a lovely Roman girl. She loved Jesus with all her heart.

But a young Roman wanted to marry her. She told him she belonged to Our Lord alone. At first he and his brother were very angry. They tried to force marriage on her. But when the young man walked toward Cecilia, he saw her strong, beautiful Guardian Angel standing at her side.

The young man at once became a Christian. So did his brother.

The Roman soldiers came and took all three of them prisoners.

They cried, "Offer sacrifice to our gods."

But Cecilia, though just a young woman, spoke for all of them.

"We love and serve only the true God." she answered.

So all three went to Heaven together in martyrdom.

Just a few years ago, Cecilia's body was found in its grave in Rome. Though she had been dead for almost eighteen hundred years, her body was still fresh and sweet and beautiful as if she were asleep. Thus God protects those who love Him.

Her Feast is: November 22nd.

Saint Charbel
Hermit

Yussef was only three years old when his father died. His mother taught him about prayer and fasting and daily Mass. His uncle helped take care of the family.

Yussef helped in the fields which gave him time alone with God to pray.

When he was 23 years old, he wanted to give his life completely to God. He went to the Monastery of St. Maron in Lebanon and became a monk.

He was given the name Charbel and after he became a priest, he moved to a Hermitage near the Monastery.

He worked hard planting crops and he celebrated daily Mass and adoration of the Eucharist. He ate only one meal each day and prayed that people in the outside world would turn to God. He was a very holy man.

After Charbel died and was buried, bright lights glowed around his grave and people began praying to him to ask God to help them with their sicknesses and their problems. People came to visit the place where he was buried and many miracles happened.

His Feast Day is December 24th.

Saint Charles
Borromeo

Charles Borromeo was a rich Italian young man. His family was noble. His uncle was Pope Pius IV.

But more than anything, Charles wanted to be a good priest. At that time the Protestant churches had just begun. They did not believe in the Mass or the Blessed Sacrament.

Besides, because of war and disease, Italy badly needed good priests and fine Catholics.

So Charles became a priest. The Pope made him a Bishop very young. At once he worked hard for the poor. He took care of the sick in their own homes. When he preached, thousands came to hear him.

But often he sat by the road and taught one poor man his prayers.

He loved the Church because Christ loved it. He brought thousands back to Mass and Holy Communion. He built fine seminaries for priests, and schools for children.

In the end, a terrible sickness came to Milan, his city. Charles nursed the sick himself. He laid them on his own bed.

He died of the sickness, a martyr of charity.

His Feast is November 4th.

Saint Christopher
The Christ Bearer

Saint Christopher was a giant and very strong. He was a very brave soldier. "I will serve only the strongest men in the world," he said. So he fought in the army of a great, strong king. But one day the soldier saw the king tremble and grow pale. The king was afraid of Satan. The thought of the Devil frightened him.

So Christopher, whose name was then Offero, went to serve the Devil. But soon he found that the Devil was afraid of someone too. Oh, he was very strong, but he was afraid of Jesus Christ.

"I will serve Jesus Christ," said Christopher.

So he went to a river where many travellers came. He carried them across on his strong shoulders. Some day, he thought, Jesus Christ might come that way.

Then one day a little Boy came to the river.

Christopher hoisted the Boy on his shoulders. He was very light. But as they crossed the river, He got heavier and heavier. "Who are You?" asked the giant. "I am Jesus Christ," said the Boy. "You looked for Me."

The giant was very happy. He became a Christian. His name became Christopher; that means, the man who carried Christ.

He is the patron saint of travellers. Especially he is the patron of those who travel in automobiles.

His traditional Feast is July 25th.

Saint Clare

Franciscan

Sometimes we call her Saint Clare. Sometimes, Saint Clara or Saint Claire.

Her mother and father were very rich. She lived in a beautiful Italian palace.

But she listened to a man named Saint Francis of Assisi. He was very like Christ. He loved God. He wanted to be poor. He hoped to save the world from sin.

So, when her parents said she could not be a nun, Clare ran away. She cut her hair. She put on old clothes with a rope for her belt. In a little hut, she took her sister, then her mother and some friends. She began the sisters known as the Poor Clares.

All day long these sisters pray for sinners. They love God for those who do not love Him. They do penance so that men and women will not lose their souls.

Once the army of men who hated Christ came to Assisi. They meant to destroy the city.

Saint Clare carried the Blessed Sacrament outside the convent. Only her sisters were around her. But the great army saw her coming. They turned and fled in panic.

She had saved the city.

Her Feast is August 11th.

Saint Clotilde
Queen of France

Once upon a time there was a very beautiful princess. Her name was Clotilde. She lived in what is now France.

Many kings heard of her famous beauty. Each longed to make her his wife.

For Clotilde was as good as she was beautiful.

The strongest king of those days was named Clovis the Great. He was very warlike and often cruel.

He demanded that Clotilde marry him. So she did. But she was sorry because he was not a Christian.

His sweet wife loved him very much and he loved her. So he soon became less cruel. He was more merciful to his enemies.

Soon a powerful enemy attacked him.

"I will pray to Jesus for you," Clotilde said, "and you must pray too."

So they both prayed. And Clovis won a great victory.

He was grateful to his wife and to Jesus who had helped him. He became the first Catholic king of France.

When her husband died, Clotilde spent her time in prayer and in good deeds.

Her traditional Feast is June 3rd.

Saint Colette

The Franciscan

Colette lived in dangerous times.

Three men all pretended to be the real Pope.

Many Christians did not know which was the true Pope. But Colette did.

When she was a little girl she became a sister.

Saint Francis appeared to her in a vision one day. He asked her to love God very much.

"And make your sisters good nuns," he begged her.

So she did. She showed them how happy a good nun is. She taught them how to take care of the poor and teach little children about Jesus Christ.

This little nun loved the Catholic Church very much.

So God showed her which was the right Pope.

Bravely she told the Bishops and Cardinals what to do. They followed her advice. One Pope was elected and the Church was happy again.

The devils hated her because she was so good. They feared her because she loved the Church.

So they appeared to her in ugly shapes. They played horrid tricks on her. They tempted her severely.

"Stop praying to Jesus," they cried, "and we will stop bothering you." But she only prayed the harder.

She died smiling as she was praying to God to forgive all sinners.

Her Feast is March 6th.

Saint Cyril and Methodius
Brother Saints

Cyril and Methodius were brothers born in Greece. They joined monasteries but were called out to be missionaries. They were sent to teach the Moravians about God because they knew the Slovanic language and the people could understand them. They were very successful and invented an alphabet and translated the Mass and major portions of the Bible into the people's own language. Through their hard work, they brought Christianity to many countries.

The German bishop did not like the use of the Slavonic language in the church and would not ordain the priests so that Cyril and Methodius could continue their mission. So, the two brothers went to Rome and the Pope approved the use of their language in the Liturgy and ordained their priests.

Cyril became a monk and died in Rome. Methodius went on to become Bishop of Moravia but the German king had him put in prison for two years. The Pope had him released but he had to once again fight for the right to use these people's own language for Mass.

It took him ten years to convince Pope John to allow the Slavonic language in the Mass. The last four years of his life, Methodius finished translating the entire Bible into Slavonic except for one book, Maccabees.

Their Feast is February 14th.

Saint Dominic
Great Preacher

Dominic was a fine, brave young Spaniard.

He was a smart student, too. He also loved the poor, and sold even his clothes and books to give money to those who were hungry.

In those days, evil men hated Jesus Christ and the truth. They were called Albigenses. They destroyed homes. They burned churches. They killed Catholics, especially priests and nuns.

Bravely Dominic decided to gather an army to fight them. Only his was an army of peace. He gathered fine young men and dressed them in white.

"I shall call you the Order of Preachers," he said. Nowadays we call these fine priests the Dominicans.

Dominic and his priests went everywhere and taught people the truth about Jesus Christ and goodness.

He gathered pure young women and dressed them in white too.

"You will pray for sinners," he said. These were the first Dominican nuns.

To help him win his battle of peace, Mary, our Blessed Mother, gave him a powerful weapon.

It was her Rosary. With that, Dominic and his brave men and pure women overcame the enemies of Christ and His Church.

His traditional Feast is August 4th.

Saint Dorothy
Martyr

Dorothy's Mother and Father had both been martyrs. They had bravely died for Jesus Christ.

So the soldiers came for the little girl too. They dragged her to the judge. They beat and punished her. But she was faithful to Christ.

The judge told two wicked women to take her and show her how silly it was to believe in Our Lord. Instead, she converted them and made them both Christians.

The judge was now furious. He ordered the soldiers to treat her more cruelly. She only smiled. She did not think of her pain but of the two souls she had saved.

It was mid-winter when she was put to death. There was no fruit and no flowers. A pagan lawyer who hated Christ laughed at her.

"Send me some apples or roses from Heaven, will you?" he asked.

Just before she died, a little child stood at her side with three apples and three roses. The child was an angel from Heaven.

"Take them to the lawyer," Dorothy smiled and died.

The lawyer too became a Catholic and died a martyr.

Her traditional Feast is February 6th.

Saint Edward
The Confessor

Edward was one of the greatest Kings of England. He was called the Confessor, because he confessed his belief in Jesus Christ. He admitted proudly that he was a Catholic. He ruled his Kingdom as Christ wanted it ruled. Edward never expected to be king. Indeed, when he was very young, bad men drove him away from England.

But the good people remembered him. They knew he would be a fine king.

So when he was forty years old, they brought him back. "Be our king!" they cried. And he accepted.

He was a very good king. He loved the poor. He spent his money to make them happy.

He was never proud. Instead of sitting on a throne, he walked the streets, talking with people, asking them their troubles, helping them to be happy.

He married a very good queen. They lived pure lives. People said, "There is a perfect husband and wife."

Often sick people came to him. He touched them and they were cured. All his laws were good. They helped make his people happy.

He was king for twenty four years. There were no wars. The country grew rich and happy.

Before he died, he built the Westminster Abbey.

His Feast is October 13th.

Saint Elizabeth
of Hungary

St. Elizabeth, Queen of Hungary, was only twenty-four when she died.

But what a beautiful life she had led!

Her father was a king. Her aunt was St. Hedwig.

When she was very young, she married Louis, a young nobleman, who soon became king.

She was sweet to her husband and loved her children. But she knew that queens should be very good to the poor and the sick. So she took care of them in the palace. She nursed them in the hospitals.

Her husband grew angry. "That's no work for a queen," he said.

One day she went to visit the poor. Her cloak was full of provisions. Her husband met her.

"Are you carrying food like a servant?" he cried.

He pulled open her cloak. Out fell not food but lovely red and white roses. Her husband asked her forgiveness. He knew she was a saint.

Her husband died when she was still very young. The next king treated her very badly and threw her out of her palace.

But she trusted God and God took her swiftly to His palace in Heaven.

Her Feast is November 17th.

Saint Fiacre

Gardener

Fiacre was born in Ireland and became a monk.

The people of his town found out that he grew plants and herbs that could heal and that he was a very holy man. They wanted to spend time around him but he wanted to be alone so he left Ireland and moved to France.

He had a small area of land where he gardened and soon people from all around came to him for spiritual and physical healing. As more people came, Fiacre asked the Bishop, Faro, for more land. Bishop Faro offered Fiacre as much land as he could till in one day. So for one day, Fiacre dragged his staff across the ground and a large area of land was miraculously cleared. Trees fell, weeds were removed and rocks fell over. Fiacre built a hospice there where he took care of those in need. He made a place for himself where he could pray and fast and work in his garden. Men came to join him in his work to cure those in need and they formed a monastery. He was known to cure all kinds of diseases by laying on his hands.

He made the blind see, lowered fevers and removed tumors. The plants and herbs he grew in his garden were used for medicine. This is why he is known as the patron saint of gardeners.

His Feast is August 30th.

Saint Frances
of Rome

Frances was a married saint.

She had always wanted to be a nun. But her parents wouldn't let her. They insisted she marry a wealthy Roman nobleman.

Once she was married, Frances and her husband lived forty years without a hard word or unkind deed. She was a good wife and a saintly mother.

Yet she prayed all she could. She took care of the poor, giving them even her own food. But she knew her chief duty was to take care of her house. Even prayer came second to that.

Then her troubles came. The enemies of her country captured Rome. They stole her property. They drove her husband away. They threw her son into prison. Frances was very poor. But she accepted all this as God's will.

When peace was restored, Frances started a new order of nuns.

Then her husband died. And Frances joined the nuns herself.

Often she saw her own guardian angel. When she was very good, his light was very bright. If she committed even a fault, his light faded away.

Her Feast is March 9th.

Saint Frances Xavier Cabrini
Mother Cabrini

From the time she was a very small girl Frances Cabrini wanted to be a missionary. Her home was in Italy.

When she grew up she hoped to go all over the world working for God, but there were no Sisters who did the kind of work she thought God wanted her to do.

So she began a new order of nuns.

She named it for the Sacred Heart. Things did not always go well for her, but she knew that the Sacred Heart would take care of her work.

She came to America and started hospitals, orphanages and schools in many cities for poor children.

She also went to other countries to take care of the poor people there.

She was a small frail lady but she never stopped working. She was doing it to help Jesus save souls and that made her strong. She is called an American Saint.

Her Feast is December 22nd.

Saint Francis Xavier
The Missionary

Saint Francis Xavier went to the University of Paris. He was a champion runner. He was a great athlete.

But he was a very clever student, too.

In class, he was the leader. He learned easily. He studied hard. "I want to be a great professor," he said. "I want to know all there is to know. I want people to listen when I talk. I want to write wonderful books."

Then he met Saint Ignatius Loyola.

"What good will it do you," Ignatius asked him, "if you win the whole world and then lose your soul?"

Francis thought this over. He decided he could win the world and at the same time save his soul. So he became a friend of Saint Ignatius. He became a Jesuit.

"Send me out," he said, "and I will win the world for our dear Lord."

So Ignatius sent him out as a missionary.

He went to India. He told people there about Jesus.

He went to Japan. The pagans listened. Many of them too became Catholics.

Then he wanted to go to China. Instead, he died on a little island just off the coast of China.

But he had converted thousands and thousands.

He was the greatest missionary since the days of the Apostles.

His Feast is December 3rd.

Saint Francis
of Assisi

Many people say that St. Francis was the man who was most like Our Lord.

He saw how money makes many people bad and proud. So he wanted to be as poor as Our Lord was.

He used to say, "I am married to Lady Poverty."

Far in the East are men called Moslems. They do not believe in Jesus Christ. So Francis went to visit them. And though they hated other Christians, they listened to Francis. They thought Jesus must be very fine, because Francis, His friend, was so good.

Once when Francis was praying a wonderful thing happened. God placed in his hands and feet the same marks that Our Lord carried after He was crucified. These are called Stigmata.

Francis preached about Jesus and Mary everywhere.

He built the first Christmas crib.

But so that everyone could hear about Our dear Lord, he gathered men and women to work with him. They worked among the poor people. They taught them how happy it is to be good.

They are called the Franciscans.

His Feast is October 4th.

Saint Genevieve
Patroness of Paris

Like Saint Joan of Arc, little Genevieve was a shepherdess. She tended her sheep near Paris.

One day a great saint passed by. He saw the little girl. "She is very holy," he said. "She will grow holier still." She spent her time in praying, in caring for the sick, in helping the poor.

A powerful king attacked Paris. The people were starving. Little Genevieve, quite unafraid, took some of her girl friends, and went out where the enemy could see her. They gathered food and brought it back to, the starving Parisians. No one dared to hurt her.

Another time, another general attacked Paris.

"Join with me in praying and fasting," she cried to the people. "He will not hurt us or hurt the city."

Everyone in Paris did as she said. To their delight, the general and his army packed up and left the city unharmed.

The new King of France had just become a Catholic. Clovis was his name.

He heard about Genevieve and sent for her.

"Teach me how to be a good king," he asked this little shepherdess.

Paris loved Saint Genevieve. She is the city's patroness.

Her Feast is January 3rd.

Saint George
Great Soldier and Martyr

George was a strong and brave soldier in the army of the Roman Emperor Diocletian. Because of his courage, he quickly became one of the Emperor's favorite soldiers and Diocletian made him a colonel in the army.

Diocletian was an evil leader and hated all Christians and ordered them to be put to death.

But George was a Christian and stood up against the Emperor's command. Even though he knew that he might lose everything he had gained in his rank as a colonel in the army, he went to the Emperor and told him that he was wrong to put the Christians to death.

George was cast into prison because he was a Christian and he was put on trial for his religious beliefs. George would not back down even though the Emperor had him tortured. Diocletian finally had George led through the city and killed. Because he died for his Faith, we call him a martyr.

Pictures show George riding on a horse killing a dragon which is the symbol for evil or the devil. He was a soldier for Christ who stood up and fought against a very evil ruler. He is the patron saint of soldiers.

His Feast Day is April 23rd.

Saint Gerard
The Mother Saint

Gerard was only twelve years old when his father died.

His father had been a tailor and so Gerard went to work for the tailor to help feed his family and with any money left over, Gerard fed the poor. He tried to enter the monastery but they wouldn't let him join because he was often sick. When the Redemptorists Fathers came to town to preach about their order, Gerard tried to join them but they refused him too. When they were leaving town, they told Gerard's mother to keep him locked in his room so that he would not follow them. The next morning his mother found a note on his bed that said he had gone to become a saint. The Fathers sent him on to one of their houses with a note to the head of the novices that said Gerard would be useless because he was often sick. But Gerard did more work than anyone.

He was always picked to go out to the different towns on missions because he helped people go to confession and changed their lives. Sometimes he could tell people some of the sins they should confess. He was very holy and the people in the towns loved him. One day he dropped his handkerchief in the street and a young girl picked it up and tried to give it back to him.

He told her to keep it because she may need it sometime. Years later the girl was about to have a baby and the doctor told her that she was going to die. The girl asked him to bring her the handkerchief from her dresser and when she got it she was all better and she and her baby lived. After he died, many other mothers told stories of miracles that occurred because they prayed to Gerard for help. His Feast is October 16th.

Saint Gertrude
Abbess

Sometimes men and women are so holy that Our Dear Lord comes to talk with them.

He likes to bring His Blessed Mother with Him too.

And they both tell these saints about Heaven and about the things the Holy Family did on earth.

Gertrude was a saint like this.

She was a holy nun who lived in a convent in Germany.

She was very clever. When she was a little girl she could write and speak Latin. But most of all, she wanted to know about God. So often Our Dear Lord and His Mother appeared to her.

They told her lovely secrets about life after death. They told her how safely we can all reach Heaven.

All these things Saint Gertrude wrote down in lovely books. We can still read these books.

How sweet it is to be very holy. For then Christ and Mary love to be with us.

Her Feast is November 16th.

Saint Gregory
The Pope

Young Gregory's father was very rich.

When his father died, Gregory gave all the money he inherited to the poor. Then he went to a monastery and became a monk. He prayed. He studied hard.

The Pope of those days heard about this bright young man. He called Gregory to Rome. He made him a Deacon. He sent him on important errands to kings and generals. One day in the market place, Gregory saw some slaves. They told him they were Angles.

"You should be Angels," he said.

English boys were called Angles in those days. Gregory knew they did not believe in Jesus. You see, he hoped they would be Catholics. When the Pope died, the people made Gregory the Pope.

He remembered the English boys. So he sent Saint Augustine to England to tell them about Jesus and to make them Catholics. He sent holy priests to convert the Spanish and the French. Wicked men came rushing into Italy to destroy it.

He told them about Jesus, and they became Catholics too. He wrote great books which are still read.

He taught people how to sing in Church. We still call these songs the Gregorian Chants.

He was one of the greatest Popes that ever lived.

His traditional Feast is March 12th.

Saint Helen

Queen

Helen was a British princess. She became Empress of Rome.

At first, she was not a Christian. But she was a good woman. So soon Our Lord gave her the gift of faith.

Her strongest son was named Constantine. He was a pagan too. But when he saw his Mother become a Christian, he started thinking.

When Helen was eighty years old, she went to Jerusalem. She wanted to find the Cross on which Our Lord died.

She found three crosses buried in Mount Calvary. But when the Cross of Our Lord touched a very sick woman, at once the woman was cured.

Later, Helen's son was fighting his strongest enemy. He remembered the Cross his Mother loved. He promised to become a Christian if he won.

He did win. And the Cross became the sign of victory for all the world.

So Saint Helen by her prayers and example made her son, Constantine, the first Christian ruler of the world.

Her traditional Feast is August 18th.

Saint Henry
Emperor

When Duke Henry of Bavaria was very young, he had a dream. His patron saint appeared to him and showed him the words, "After six."

The young man thought this meant he would die after six years. So he prepared for death. He lived like a saint.

Instead, after six years, he was chosen German emperor. But because for six years he had lived like a saint, he was a holy and great emperor.

He determined to rule for the glory of God and the good of his people. First he helped convert to Christ the nations near him who did not believe in the Savior.

A wicked man had driven the Pope from Rome. He was sitting on the Pope's own chair. Henry led his army against this bad man, beat him, and brought the Holy Father back to Rome.

Whenever he entered the city, his first visit was always to Christ in the Blessed Sacrament. Once Christ rewarded him wonderfully. Henry saw Jesus Himself say Mass in a great church in Rome.

Both Henry and his wife, Cunegunda, became great saints.

His traditional Feast is July 15th.

Saint Ignatius
A Martyr and a Jesuit

There are two great saints named Ignatius.

One was the Bishop of Antioch. Saint John the Apostle taught him to know and love Jesus.

The Blessed Sacrament was very dear to his heart. He was always teaching people that Jesus gave them His flesh to eat and His blood to drink.

The Roman Emperor was angry because Ignatius would not call him a god. So he dragged him to Rome.

"Let the lions devour him!" the Emperor ordered.

Ignatius was glad to die for the truth.

Jesus had given His flesh in Holy Communion for him. So he gave his flesh to the lions for love of Jesus.

The other saint who was named Ignatius was a brave soldier and was called Saint Ignatius of Loyola.

One day he was wounded badly in battle. When he was getting well, he read the Lives of the Saints.

"What they did, I can do!" he thought. And he became the brave soldier of Christ.

So he established a new Society of Priests and Brothers. He called it the Society of Jesus.

The Feast of St. Ignatius of Antioch is February 1st.

The Feast of St. Ignatius of Loyola is July 31st.

PATER MEUS
AGRICOLA
EST

92

Saint Isidore

Farmer

When Isidore was young, his parents were poor.

He had to go work on a farm for a man that he worked for the rest of his life. Isidore woke up early every morning and went to Mass before work. As he plowed the fields during the day, he prayed to God and asked his guardian angel to watch over him.

Sometimes he came to the field late because he stayed at church to pray but he miraculously finished more work than any of the other workers. Some people said they saw the angels helping him in the fields. Isidore cared for the poor and shared his food with them.

He married a girl who loved God as much as he did. They had one son who died when he was young. His wife helped him to care for the poor and help their neighbors. One day Isidore was carrying a bag of corn to the mill to be ground and saw some birds that were hungry. It was cold and snowy and he felt sad for the birds.

He opened the bag and poured half of the corn out for them to eat. The worker with him made fun of what he had done but when he got to the place to ground the corn, the bag was full and made twice the amount of meal it would usually make. Isidore loved God and all of His creation and in return God took care of him.

His Feast Day is May 15th.

Saint James
The Greater

James was one of the three Apostles Jesus kept nearest to Him. The other two were Peter and John.

Like so many of the Apostles, James was a fisherman.

He followed Our Lord up the mountain when His face became bright as the Sun.

He was in the room when Jesus brought the little dead girl back to life.

When our dear Lord suffered the Agony in the Garden, James was near Him.

He had a fierce temper which he conquered with difficulty. But he had great faith and preached powerfully. So he was called the Son of Thunder.

After Our Lord ascended into Heaven, James bravely went around telling everyone about the Savior.

King Herod was angry. He cried, "Do you believe in Jesus Christ?"

"Indeed I do," James answered at once.

So the soldiers cut off his head with a sword, and he died a martyr.

His Feast is July 25th.

Saint Jane

Frances de Chantal

Here is a wonderful saint.

She was a saint as a little girl. She was a saint as a wife. When she was a widow, she was a saint. Then she became a nun and was a saint in the convent.

When she was a very little girl, Jane Frances asked Our Lady to take care of her. Our Lady always did.

Then she married a nobleman. She made him a beautiful home. She loved her husband. She was devoted to her children.

But sorrow came to her. Her good husband died. Two children and a sister died. Her friends bothered her to marry again. She was sad and her life was very hard.

At last her children grew up. She knew that God wanted her to be a nun. So with Saint Francis de Sales she started the Visitation Order.

Her daughters, the Visitation Sisters, to this day pray, do penance, and teach children to love and serve God as Jane Frances did.

Her Feast is August 18th.

Saint Jerome
Doctor of the Church

Jerome's father sent him to Rome to study. He loved to learn Latin and Greek.

After traveling for some time, he decided to become a monk and he gave himself completely to God. He learned Hebrew so that he could study the Scriptures in the original language and he translated some of the great works of previous writers from Greek to Latin.

He was ordained a priest and Pope Damascus called him back to Rome to be his secretary. Jerome wrote many commentaries on the Scriptures and revised the Latin New Testament, based on the Greek. His version of the Bilble became the official translation, being closer to the first writings.

After Pope Damascus died, Jerome moved to Bethlehem where he started a monastery and lived the rest of his life studying and teaching and writing.

Jerome defended the faith his entire life. In his writings, he helped all who would listen to understand more about the Bible. He is the patron of scholars and those who study scripture.

His Feast Day is September 30th.

Saint Joan
of Arc

Joan of Arc did not start out to be a soldier. She was just a simple little shepherd girl.

She lived quietly in France with her family. But she loved God very much. And she wanted to see her country free and strong.

At that time, her country was fighting the English. The English were winning everywhere.

Suddenly Joan heard the voices of angels and saints speaking to her. "Go and save your country," they commanded her.

At first she was afraid. But then she knew God wished it. So she wore armor and rode a horse into battle.

The poor French king had not even his crown. The armies were afraid.

But Joan led them to victory. She crowned the king in his own palace. Then she said, "My work is done. Let me go back to my sheep."

But the king would not let her. Instead, her friends let the enemy capture her. And they burned her to death at the stake.

Joan's soul went straight to God. Her work was done. The French had won their country back.

And Joan is the patroness of soldiers who fight for their land.

Her Feast is: May 30th.

Saint John

The Beloved Apostle

John was a young fisherman in the Holy Land.

One day, our dear Lord said to him, "Come and follow Me." Quickly he left family, boat, everything, and became an Apostle.

He saw Our Lord heal the sick and raise the dead. He heard the wonderful things Our Lord taught. He loved Jesus very much.

He sat next to Jesus the night when He gave His Apostles their First Communion.

Then when the other Apostles ran away from Calvary, John stayed on beside Mary. And Jesus gave this young man Mary for his Mother.

He became a great bishop. He wrote the Fourth Gospel and beautiful letters.

He took care of Mary after Jesus ascended into Heaven.

The Romans tried to kill him by boiling him in oil. But Jesus protected him. He was not even hurt.

Because he was very pure, Jesus loved him best of all the Apostles.

His Feast is December 27th.

Saint John
of God

John left home at a young age and worked as a shepherd. The man he worked for wanted him to marry his daughter but John wanted to find his way in the religious life.

John went through many tough times before he found what God wanted him to do. He was a soldier in the Spanish army. He worked loading ships and later selling books and holy pictures. He even opened his own bookstore for a while. But John began spending more and more time with the sick and the poor.

He was put in the hospital for a time and while he was there he helped others who were sick like him. When he got out of the hospital, he decided to keep helping the sick and the poor. He first worked helping the poor people living in the streets and later opened a house for the sick and the poor. He begged on the streets for beds and medicine and food.

One night the hospital in the city caught on fire and he went and rescued all the patients who could not save themselves. He passed through the flames without getting burned. This is why John of God is one of the patron saints of firefighters as well as booksellers, hospitals and the sick.

His Feast day is March 8th.

Saint John
of the Cross

John was the son of a poor silk weaver. His father died when he was young and his mother and brother could hardly make enough money to feed the family. John went to a poor school and worked very hard to do well but when he was sent out to work, he seemed unable to learn. So, he had to work with the poor in the hospital and go to a school run by the Jesuits. He became a priest and was told in prayer that he would serve God by bringing back the original rules of the Carmelite order.

He worked with Teresa of Avila and opened many monasteries with the old, harder ways. Many of the other brothers of his order did not like the work he was doing and had him put in prison. He sat for nine months in a dark cell that was barely large enough for his body. During his time of pain and suffering, he wrote most of his famous poems. John escaped from this prison by tying rags together and making a long rope and sliding down the monastery wall. He found his way to a convent where the nuns nursed him back to health and wrote down many of the words he told them which would later become his books.

He returned to work with Teresa. John wrote many books and was one of the greatest poets of the Church.

After Teresa died, everything John had worked for was taken away and he was put into one of the poorest monasteries where he was mistreated and became very sick. John continued to pray and show kindness and charity to all who mistreated him. By the time he died, those who were around him believed in his holiness. His Feast is December 14th.

Saint John
The Baptiste de la Salle

John was from a wealthy family. He began his studies toward the priesthood at a young age and was ordained when he was 27 years old. He had a good life at the Cathedral in France and was very content.

John was asked to help open a free school for the poor in his city and he opened not just one school, but two. But, he noticed that the teachers were not very good in these schools so he opened a school to train teachers.

His easy life soon became difficult but he believed that it was God's will to help these poor children and their teachers. He sold all his worldly goods and quit his work at the Cathedral to donate all his money and time to education.

He started his own community called the Brothers of the Christian Schools. They opened the first training college for teachers and vowed to provide free education to the poor for the rest of their lives.

He said that every person was worthy of respect because they were made in the image of God. He asked teachers to study the scriptures and to carry a New Testament with them always so that they could be examples of Christ to their students.

He taught the importance of prayer and Communion.
His Feast is April 7th.

Saint Joseph
Foster Father

Joseph was a poor carpenter of Nazareth.

Yet he came from the royal family of David. And he was pure and good and hard working.

God knew He could trust Joseph, so He chose him for a most important task. He became the husband of Mary and the Foster Father of Our Lord.

So he protected Mary on the way to Bethlehem. He was present on the first Christmas. He led Mary and Jesus safely into Egypt when Herod was trying to kill the Child. Later he worked for them. He made them a sweet little home. He earned money to give them their food and clothing.

When Jesus was a big boy, Joseph taught Him the carpenter's trade.

Joseph did not live to see Jesus become great and famous. Instead he died happily with Mary at his bedside, and Jesus blessing him.

He worked very hard to make life safe and happy for Jesus and Mary.

So Jesus has made him the Protector of the Whole Church. His Feast is March 19th.

Saint Jude

Martyr

Saint Jude is also called Saint Jude Thaddeus. He had three brothers. Their names were Saint James the Less, Saint Simeon of Jerusalem, and Joseph. Saint Jude and his three brothers were brethren of Jesus. Saint Jude Thaddeus was one of the twelve apostles of Jesus. His kinship to our Saviour filled him with joy. He had the ardor of holy zeal and love. He was ready to sacrifice and to suffer for the Master's sake. He wanted to tell all the people the truth about Jesus. After the Lord ascended into Heaven, Saint Jude set out with his companions to preach the Gospel. With only the word of God and his spirit he won out over evil. Everywhere he went people listened to him. He traveled far, in Judaea, in Samaria, in Syria and in Mesopotamia. In his travels he met Saint Simeon and they preached together. Everywhere he went he taught people to be humble. He taught them to be meek. He taught them to pray. He taught them to love God. He said, "We owe God praise and thanks for His endless mercy." Saint Jude wrote a long letter. This letter was to all the Jewish converts, among whom he preached. The letter is called "The Epistle to the Hebrew Christians." Saint Jude chose to suffer rather than give up his faith. While he was in Mesopotamia he converted many sinners. His enemies put him to death. He suffered martyrdom. Saint Jude is regarded as the special patron of the sick, especially those whose cases seem to be helpless. His Feast is October 28th.

Saint Julia

Virgin Martyr

Julia was a rich noblewoman. She lived in North Africa. The armies that hated Christ captured her country. Julia was seized and sold as a slave.

A rich merchant bought her. So this sweet, gentle, well educated woman did the hardest work of his house without pay. But she smiled and was brave. She prayed constantly to Jesus whom she loved.

Some time later, her master took her to a pagan place where people were praying to false gods.

Julia refused to have part in it.

One of the rich Romans was furious. He cried out, "That slave girl is a Christian. She should die." Her owner protected her.

But when her owner was asleep, the Roman seized her. "Pray to my gods," he cried. "I will set you free if you do." "Everyone is free," she answered, "if he loves, Jesus Christ."

So the Roman beat her, nailed her to a cross, and she died a saint and martyr.

Her Feast is May 23rd.

Kateri Tekakwitha
Native American

Tekakwitha was only four when her father, her mother and her brother died from smallpox.

She was left partially blind and her face scarred. Her two aunts and her uncle took care of her. She worked in the fields and helped around the house. She loved to go to the forest and collect firewood. One day a Jesuit priest came to the village and taught her about Jesus.

When she was baptized, she took the name Kateri.

Her family was not happy about her being a Christian and refused to let her eat on Sundays when she would not work.

They began to make life very hard for her. She ran away to Canada and lived in a Catholic mission.

She spent time in the woods and made crosses out of sticks to mark places where she prayed. Kateri went to Mass every day and fasted, keeping her life focused on her Faith. She took care of the sick and loved to tell stories about the love of Jesus. When she was twenty one, she made her First Communion.

She wanted to start a convent in Canada but she was too sick. She died when she was only twenty four years old. When she died, the scars on her face disappeared and she was beautiful. She became known as the "Lily of the Mohawks".

Her Feast Day is July 14th.

Saint Lawrence
Martyr

Lawrence was a fine young Roman.

He was chosen a deacon. That meant that it was his work to care for the sick and the poor.

But the Romans thought he was the treasurer of the Church.

So they took him prisoner. "Show us the treasures of the Church," they cried.

Lawrence had a great sense of humor.

"Gladly," he answered.

The Romans hurried after him, expecting to find gold and precious stones. Instead, he led them to the hospital where the poor and the sick lived.

"Here are the treasures of the Church," he cried. They were furious. But Lawrence knew how God loves the poor and needy.

In the end, the Romans put him to death. They laid him on a gridiron over a fire. But even there, Lawrence could joke.

"Turn me over," he cried, as the fire burned, "for I think I am done on this side."

Even in his pain, God gave Lawrence deep happiness. His Feast is August 10th.

Saint Leo the Great
The Pope

The name Leo means the Lion.

And Saint Leo, the Pope, was a lion in bravery.

The Vandals and Huns, two terrible races, were fighting the Christians of Europe.

Besides this, evil men were teaching people lies about Jesus. They were saying what was not true and getting the people confused. Leo became Pope. He had been a smart and wise young man. Now he had to be a brave and very wise Pope. First he went everywhere teaching the truth about our dear Lord. He called together all the wise priests and bishops of the Church. This was the great Council of Chalcedon.

They talked and studied and listened.

And they went home to teach their people the truth. So people did not believe the evil men any more when they lied about the Savior.

But the Vandals and Huns kept coming. They burned cities. They murdered people everywhere.

All alone, without weapons, Leo went out to meet them.

Their leader Attila was called the Awful Scourge.

But when he saw Leo he ordered his armies to cease fighting. Instead of destroying Rome, they turned and went away. The Pope had saved Europe.

His traditional Feast is April 11th.

Saint Louis
The King of France

Louis was a fine, strong, pure boy. His mother taught him to hate sin. Her name was Blanche.

"I love you, my son," she said; "but I would rather see you dead than have you commit one mortal sin."

He remembered this all his life. He was made King of France. He determined to be a good and generous king. So he established great schools.

He made wise laws. He gave money freely to the poor. He stopped evil men who were teaching lies to the people. Each day he found time to hear two Masses. He prayed far into the night.

In those days, the Moslems hated Christians. They were trying to destroy the Christian countries. They had great armies. They sailed powerful fleets. It looked as if they would win.

But Louis made sure they would not.

He gathered a great army and marched out to fight them. He was so brave and fine that the Moslems respected him. Some of them asked him to be their king. Yet God did not wish him to win with the sword. He really seemed to lose that war. Only he didn't. The Moslems never conquered Christian lands. Other brave men fought as King Louis had done.

Europe was saved for Christ.

His Feast is August 25th.

Saint Louis Marie
de Montfort

Louis was devoted to Jesus as a child. He prayed in front of the Blessed Sacrament and loved to go to Mass and pray the rosary.

He and some of his friends helped the sick and the poor and read to them when they were not in school.

He decided to become a priest and on his way to Paris where he would study, gave away all of his belongings and traded his clothes with those of a beggar.

He became a priest and for a while worked in the hospital chapel. But Louis wanted to go out and preach to the people in the cities.

He wanted to give missions and teach about Mary and the rosary and the love of God.

Many areas he went to did not like him and he was made to leave. He went to Rome to ask the Pope what to do and the Pope sent him back to France to be a missionary.

He wrote books about the Blessed Mother and formed a group called the Company of Mary.

His Feast Day is April 28th.

Saint Lucy
Martyr

When Lucy was a little girl in Italy, her Mother was very ill.

"Let's pray," said Lucy, "and I know you'll get well."

So they prayed at the little church of Saint Agatha in Rome. Suddenly Saint Agatha appeared to Lucy. "Lucy, my sister!" she said to the little girl; "your Mother will be well. But you will die a martyr for Christ."

Next morning, her Mother was well.

Lucy was very rich. In gratitude she gave her money to the poor. Then she became a nun.

It happened that a young man who did not believe in Christ loved Lucy. He wanted her to marry him. When he heard she was a nun, he was furious.

He ran to the Roman Judges. "Lucy is a Christian," he said. The soldiers seized her. They threw her into a raging fire. But the flames did not hurt her. God protected her pure body.

So the soldiers plunged a sword into her heart.

And her pure soul went straight to Heaven.

Her Feast is December 13th.

Saint Luke
The Evangelist

Saint Luke studied medicine when he was a young man and became a great doctor.

He was also a skillful painter.

One day he heard about Jesus Christ. He knew that Jesus was the Great Physician. He was sure that Jesus was the God who had made all the beautiful world.

So Saint Luke followed Jesus as His disciple.

He was very close to Saint Paul and travelled with him. He was a clever writer. So he wrote down all that the Apostles did.

This book we call the Acts of the Apostles.

Then he went to see Our Lady. He asked her all about the Baby Jesus. He wrote what she told him in the Gospel According to Saint Luke.

He asked the other Apostles what they knew about Jesus, and their stories are told in his Gospel.

He travelled with Saint Paul all over the world.

He told people that although he could heal their bodies, only Jesus could heal their souls.

He painted a lovely picture of the Blessed Virgin.

We still have copies of it.

In the end, the pagans of Greece killed him because they hated Jesus.

His Feast is October 18th.

Saint Margaret
Mary

We all know how much God loves us. He created us out of nothing. He died for our sakes. He stays with us in the Blessed Sacrament.

But men and women forget God so quickly.

He asks them to love Him. Instead they love all kinds of sinful and silly things.

Once upon a time, there was a very holy nun named Sister Margaret Mary.

She loved Our dear Lord with all her heart. She was sorry that everyone did not love Him too.

One day He appeared to her. He showed her His Sacred Heart.

"Behold the Heart that has loved men so much," He said. And He asked her to tell others about His love for them. So Margaret Mary told everyone about the Sacred Heart. She loved Jesus Christ with all her heart herself. She brought millions to love Him too.

She is the saint of Sacred Heart of Jesus.

Her Feast is October 16th.

Saint Maria Goretti
Youthful Martyr

Maria Goretti was born into a poor family.

When her father died, her mother had to go each day and work in the fields to support the family and Maria had to do all the cooking and the cleaning and the caring for the other children. She was always joyful in her work and made time to go into town and receive weekly communion.

She prayed the rosary with the other children and filled her day with work and prayer.

Her family shared a place to live with a man and his son, Alessandro because they were so poor.

Alessandro said improper things to Maria but Maria always got away from him. Finally one day, he attacked her and when she pushed him away and told him that God would not want this, he stabbed her many times.

Maria was taken to the hospital and before she died, she told the parish priest that she forgave Alessandro.

Alessandro was not sorry for what he had done to Maria until one day, while in prison, he had a dream. Maria came to him and gave flowers and from that day on, he was changed forever. When he got out of prison, he went to Maria's mother and asked her to forgive him and she did.

Her Feast is July 6th.

Saint Martha
Sister of Mary Magdalen

Often our dear Lord was tired.

Often He grew weary when wicked men hated Him and tried to capture Him.

He would then go for a visit to His friends.

His friends were Lazarus and Mary and Martha. They had a sweet and peaceful house in Bethany, not far from Jerusalem.

When He came to this house, He was happy.

Lazarus talked to Him. Mary sat at His feet and listened and loved Him.

But Martha was a busy little housekeeper.

She prepared the meals for our dear Lord.

When Lazarus, their brother, died, she and Mary sent for Jesus. All they said was, "The man You love is sick."

Jesus came Himself. In a wonderful miracle, He raised Lazarus from the dead. He gave their brother back to his sisters, Mary and Martha.

Martha was present on Calvary when Jesus died.

She helped prepare His body for burial.

She saw Him after He rose on Easter Sunday.

Later she and her brother and sister went to France. They told the French about Jesus. Many of the Frenchmen and women believed and became Christians.

Her Feast is July 29th.

Saint Martin
Bishop

The father and mother of Martin did not believe in God.

So when Martin wanted to become a Christian, they wouldn't let him. Instead, his father put him into the army when he was only fifteen.

Martin was a good soldier. Though most of the soldiers were not Christians, he loved Our Lord.

One winter night, Martin met a poor beggar, freezing in the snow. Martin had no money, so he took his sword, cut his cloak in half and gave one half to the beggar.

That night, Our Lord came to him wearing the half cloak. He heard Jesus say to the angels,

"Look; though Martin is not yet baptized, he gave Me his garment."

So Martin became a Christian and converted his parents too.

Because he was brave and strong, the people asked him to stop being a soldier and become their bishop. He did. He is one of the great apostles of France.

His traditional Feast is November 12th.

Saint Mary of Egypt
Who Had Been a Sinner

When she was a very little girl, Mary of Egypt was a great sinner.

Almost everyone heard about her. For she was very beautiful. She led so many people into sin. She was very bad. One day a crowd of people took ship for Jerusalem.

The king had just found the Cross on which our Lord was hung. Mary went along because she thought it fun to travel. She did not care about the Cross.

But when they came to Jerusalem, she went with the rest to the church. Inside was the Cross. She tried to enter. She could not. Some unseen force held her as if she were chained.

Suddenly, she knew how wicked she was.

She turned and saw a picture of Our Lady.

"Mary," she cried, "Mary Magdalen saw the Cross. Please let me stand beside that other sinful woman."

And she walked into the church. She knew that her sins had nailed Jesus to that Cross. She fell on her knees and cried and cried, repenting of all her sins.

Then she went out into the desert. For years she lived alone. She prayed. She did penance for her sin.

In the end, a holy man found her body on the sands. He buried the sinner who had become a saint.

Her Feast is April 9th.

Saint Mary
Magdalen

Once upon a time, Mary Magdalen was a great sinner.

You see, she was very beautiful. So people paid her compliments. They ran after her and made her vain. She forgot that God gave her all her beauty. She loved rich clothes and fine jewels too much. She wanted to be popular at all costs.

So she sinned. And she was very unhappy.

Then one day, she saw Jesus, Our Lord.

He looked at her and showed her how sorry He was about her sin.

Right away, she knew how ugly sin was. She followed Jesus into the house of some rich men. Though they laughed at her, she knelt at His feet. She washed His feet with tears. She wiped them with her hair. She covered them with perfume.

She did this to show how sorry she was.

From that time on, she loved only Our Lord. She did not sin again. On Calvary, she stayed with Him until He died. After His resurrection, He showed Himself to her.

Then, when He rose into Heaven, Mary Magdalen ran off into the desert. She wanted to spend all her time thinking of Him, praying to Him, and loving Him with all her heart.

Her Feast is July 22nd.

Saint Matilda

The Queen

Matilda's father, a Saxon count, was named Theodoric. Matilda's parents wanted her to be pious. They placed her in the Monastery of Exford, where her grandmother was the Abbess. There Matilda worked and prayed. She studied hard. She loved her work. She loved her parents. She loved her prayer and her spiritual reading. She became a model of virtue. Matilda's parents gave her in marriage. Her husband became the German King and Matilda the Queen. She was a good queen. While her husband went to war and enlarged his kingdom, Matilda won victories over spiritual enemies. She knew this was more worthy of a Christian. She was a pious queen. She helped the sick. She taught ignorant people about Jesus and helped them became Catholics. She spent much time in prayer and meditation, not only during the day, but far into the night. Finally, her husband helped her in her pious work. When Matilda's husband died, she called the priest to offer holy sacrifice for his soul. She cut off the jewels she wore. This was a pledge that she gave up, from that moment on, all pomp of the world. Once there was a contest between Matilda's sons, Otho and Henry. Matilda favored Henry, who was the younger son. For this fault, Matilda atoned by severe penance. Matilda founded many churches and five monasteries. Her great pleasure was to teach the poor and ignorant how to pray. Matilda taught her people how to seek true virtue. "The beginning," she said, "is to want it and to ask it of God." Her feast is March 14th.

Saint Matthew
Writer of the Gospel

Once upon a time there was a tax gatherer named Levi. The Jews did not like him. He took their tax money and gave it to the Romans. But Levi was not a bad man. He only did what he thought was his duty.

One day Jesus saw him. He saw good in him that others did not see. "Come and follow Me!" Jesus said quietly to the tax gatherer.

Levi looked up in surprise. He had never seen such a wonderful Man before. Why, it would be the greatest honor to be one of His followers!

Instantly he got up. He left his table with all the money on it. He went after our Lord. And Jesus made him one of His twelve Apostles.

He changed his name to Matthew. He wrote the wonderful Gospel According to Saint Matthew.

He saw all that Jesus did. He heard all that Jesus said. He walked with Him and grew to love Him more and more. To make sure that the world would never forget Jesus, Matthew wrote all this down in his beautiful Gospel. Gospel, you know, means Good News.

He died a blessed martyr.

With Saint Mark, Saint Luke and Saint John, he is one of the Four Evangelists.

His Feast is September 21st.

Saint Michael
Archangel

Saint Michael is one of the Archangels. He is a warrior of God. Once upon a time long ago, the bad angels made war in Heaven. They cried, "We will not serve!" They raised the red flag. They tried to drive God from the Heavenly City.

But Michael led the armies of the good angels. He drove out the evil army. He knelt before God and cried that God was his only King.

So God made him the General of His armies.

All through history, Michael has fought the battle of God. He is the Devil's strong enemy. He is the friend and protector of all those who love God and follow Jesus Christ. He protected the Chosen People, the Jews, in their wars against their enemies. He is always on the side that is right and good.

In the end of the world, a bad man named Antichrist will come. He will make war on Christ and the good people. But Michael and his army will drive him from the world.

That is why we pray after Mass, "Saint Michael, the Archangel, defend us in the day of battle."

His Feast is September 29th.

Saint Monica
Mother of Saint Augustine

Monica was a lovely young Roman girl.

She was wonderfully pure and good. She loved Jesus very much. But her father loved money and power.

So he made her marry a young Roman who was very rich. Monica worried about her dear husband. She prayed hard that he would become a Catholic. She set him a good example. And a year before he died, he asked to be baptized.

But Augustine, her son, was her real worry.

Like his father, he did not care for the Catholic faith, and he led a wild and wicked life.

"I wish you would stop praying for me," he told her. But Monica prayed and prayed.

"Don't worry," a holy priest told her, "your son cannot be lost, not after all your prayers and tears."

So Monica followed Augustine to Rome. To her joy, she found that he had completely changed his life. He was a Catholic. He had given up his sins and his evil companions.

She thanked God. She died in peace knowing that her son was going to be a great saint and a great teacher and writer of Catholic truth.

Her Feast is August 27th.

Saint Patrick
of Ireland

Patrick's name was a very noble one. It was taken from a Latin name that meant "a nobleman."

Everyone loves Patrick, so many countries say he was born there. But wherever he was born, he became the friend of all and the Apostle of Ireland.

The Irish in those days did not know about Jesus and Mary. Patrick felt very sorry for them.

He studied hard, and became a priest and a bishop.

The Pope sent him to Ireland to make it Catholic. The people of Ireland welcomed him with joy. The kings sat and listened to him. All the soldiers and colleens asked to be baptized.

He taught them about the Blessed Trinity by showing them how the shamrock had three leaves yet was one plant. He drove all evils out of Ireland as if they were snakes. Soon he built churches and schools everywhere. And Saint Brigid worked for the women while Saint Patrick worked for the men.

Since Saint Patrick's time, the Irish have carried the love of Jesus and Mary all over the world. That's why everyone loves Saint Patrick and keeps his feast day.

His Feast is March 17th.

Saint Paul

Apostle

At first his name was Saul. He hated Jesus Christ and all who believed in Him.

He helped the men who killed Saint Stephen, the first martyr.

Next he got an order from the judges to arrest Christians everywhere and put them to death.

But as he rode away to do this, a light struck him from his horse. The voice of Jesus called him. Saul was deeply sorry. He believed in Jesus Christ. He became one of His greatest Apostles.

He travelled on land and sea to tell people about Our Lord. He taught the simple. He talked to the learned. He was shipwrecked. He was thrown into prison. But nothing stopped him from preaching Christ and His Cross. Thousands believed in Jesus because of this great man. God changed his name to Paul. He wrote beautiful letters called Epistles.

In the end, he was killed with Saint Peter in Rome.

Saint Peter and Paul are both buried in the great Church of Saint Peter.

His traditional Feast is June 30th.

Saint Peter

Apostle

Simon was a fine fisherman when Jesus called him to be an Apostle.

"I will make you a fisher of men," said Jesus.

Later he became the Rock, for he was brave and strong. But often he boasted and ran into temptation.

Our Lord made him His special friend. He explained everything important to him. One night, He even let Simon walk on the water. But when Simon grew afraid, Our Lord had to rescue him.

Then one day, Simon made a great act of faith in Christ. Our Lord changed his name to Peter, which means The Rock. He made him the Head of His Church. Peter was the first pope.

Yet when Our Lord was arrested, Peter was afraid. He told everyone he was not an Apostle.

But when he wept bitterly, Jesus forgave him. He made him chief Shepherd of His flock.

Peter ruled the Church bravely. In the end, he died nailed to a cross, upside down.

His Feast is June 29th.

Saint Philip Neri
The Cheerful Saint

When Philip Neri was a young boy he lived in Rome. He had a terrible temper. He was afraid that some day he would flare up and hurt some one badly.

So he set himself to cure his temper.

He determined always to be cheerful. He learned to smile all the time. He loved to laugh. He was always pleasant. People loved just to see him and have him speak to them. Especially he loved the Holy Spirit.

Indeed, once the Holy Spirit was seen to come down upon the young Philip. He shone with the light of the Third Person of the Trinity.

Philip became a priest. He started a little church in which he gathered friends. They prayed together. They sang together. He said Mass for them. They walked in happy processions through the streets. They crowned the statue of Our Lady.

The little church was called the Oratory. That means, it was a lovely place to pray. People came to him sad. He sent them away happy. They came with their sins. He sent them away pure in soul.

Children followed him. Sinners saw how lovely it is not to sin. He made evil men love God. He taught everyone the happiness of goodness.

They called him the Apostle of Rome.

His Feast is May 26th.

Saint Pius X
Pope

When he was a boy Joseph Sarto was called Bepi. He lived in Italy. His family was very poor.

Bepi studied hard and when he grew up he became a priest. He loved God so much that he loved everyone just as God said we should.

He became a Bishop and when he was elected Pope he took the name Pius X.

He did many wonderful things for children.

He said that they should all be taught the Catechism so that they would know what the Church teaches.

He said that they should make their First Communion as soon as they knew right from wrong and that they should receive Holy Communion often.

Pius X's motto was "to restore all things in Christ" and that is what he spent his life trying to do.

His Feast is August 20th.

Saint Raphael
Archangel

Raphael was one of the seven archangels whose story we read about in the Bible. Tobit was a rich man who believed in the Lord. He turned blind and as he suffered he asked the Lord to let him die.

He remembered a lot of money that he had left in a far away land and sent his son, Tobiah, to go and bring it back. As Tobiah traveled, Raphael joined him and helped him along the way but Tobiah did not know that he was an angel. Tobiah was attacked by a giant fish and Raphael told him which parts of the fish to keep for medicine to be used later. When they got to the place his father sent him, Tobiah met Sarah who had been married seven times and whose husbands had all been killed by evil. Sarah had prayed to the Lord to relieve her suffering and the Lord sent Raphael who told Tobiah to marry Sarah and remove the evil one once and for all with the parts of the fish he had kept for healing.

Tobiah returned to his father Tobit with his new wife. He rubbed his father's eyes with the parts of the fish Raphael had made him keep and Tobit could see again.

Raphael then told them all that he was the archangel sent down from heaven to save them because they had prayed to the Lord for healing.

Raphael then returned to heaven.

His Feast is September 29th.

Saint Rita

Saint of the Impossible

When Rita was a little girl, she wanted to be a Sister. Instead, her Mother and Father made her marry a cruel, bad tempered husband.

But though he was unkind to her, Rita was a good wife. She had twin boys whom she loved very much.

But her husband had many enemies. One day, some of these men killed him. Her sons, now young men, were very angry.

"We will kill the men who murdered our Father," they cried. This is revenge and it is wrong.

Rita did not want them to commit mortal sin. She loved them. But she prayed to God to let them die rather than to commit a murder. Shortly after, God let them die. But first they confessed and received Holy Communion so that they went to Heaven.

Then Rita became an Augustinian nun.

During her life and after her death, she worked many miracles.

The Spaniards, because of her wonderful deeds, call her The Sweet Saint of the Impossible.

Her Feast is May 22nd.

Saint Robert

The Monk

Robert was a young monk who lived in England.

He heard that a group of holy young men wanted to love God very much. They wanted to be especially good to sinners. So he left his comfortable home and joined them. Soon other brave young men came. Together they built a beautiful monastery. There the poor could come for food. England had few hotels in those days. So travellers could stay over night in Robert's monastery. He gathered boys and girls to teach them about Jesus. He welcomed the sick and took care of them in his hospital. He never ate until the poor were fed. He gave away his own clothes. He sat up all night long to care for the sick. Once, as he was sitting at dinner, a friend gave him bread sweetened with honey.

But through the window, he saw a poor man. He picked up the bread and honey, placed it on a plate, and carried it to the poor man.

Next day, as he sat at dinner, the plate appeared in the air. It was bright and shining like gold. Then the monks knew that the poor man to whom Robert had given the bread and honey was Christ Himself.

When Robert died, his soul, like a bright ball of fire, went straight up into heaven. The monks heard God's voice saying, "Enter into heaven!"

His Feast is June 7th.

Saint Rose
of Viterbo

Saint Rose was only eighteen when she died.

But she was already a holy and a famous person.

As soon as she could walk, she toddled straight to Jesus in the Tabernacle.

As soon as she could talk, she talked about Jesus and heaven and God.

There was a wicked king named Frederick in those days. He hated the Pope and made war on him.

One day some of his friends came to her city. They made speeches against the Pope. They threatened to do wicked things to him.

Little Rose was only ten years old.

Without fear, she rushed into the public square. She pushed the wicked men aside. She stood before the people of her city.

"Do not listen to these men," she cried. "The Pope is the Vicar of Jesus Christ. Love him and protect him."

The people were amazed at this little girl.

But they followed her and were true to the Pope.

When still a little girl, she became a nun.

Then she went to a little convent in her city. She prayed. She cared for the poor.

She died, and her body after death remained beautiful and fragrant.

Her traditional Feast is September 4th.

Saint Rose

of Lima

This little girl is an American saint.

She was born in Lima in Peru. Columbus had discovered America less than one hundred years before.

Her name was really Isabel. But she was so beautiful that people called her Rose.

Her parents were poor. So little Rose became a maid servant.

Everybody noticed how beautiful she was. That made her afraid. Perhaps her good looks might lead her into sin. So she cut her lovely hair. She worked until her hands were rough. She wore old, unattractive clothes. She wanted her soul to be beautiful. Only God could see that.

Then she decided to become a Dominican nun.

So many people around her were sinful. Rose wanted to do penance for their sins. She lived in a little hut. She slept on the floor. She begged God to forgive sinners.

When the fleet of her country's enemies attacked Peru, her prayers drove them away and saved her city.

When she died, all Peru wept for the little Rose they loved.

Her Feast is August 23rd.

Saint Scholastica
The Benedictine

Saint Benedict was the first of the holy monks.

Saint Scholastica was his beloved sister.

He built monasteries for holy men. She built convents for holy women.

Those were evil days and were full of dangers for good women.

Bands of wicked soldiers roamed all over the world.

So Saint Scholastica built lovely convents. They were full of peace. Women came there and were safe.

Saint Benedict loved his sister very much.

One day, he sat and talked with her about God.

Night came and he said, "I must go back to my home." "Please don't go," she said. For she knew she was going to die.

When her brother, Benedict, insisted upon leaving, she bowed her head and prayed.

Suddenly a great storm burst. The wind blew. The rain fell. The lightning flashed. Benedict could not go back. So all night long they sang together, they prayed together, they talked about God.

Three days later, Scholastica died. And Benedict saw her soul going up to heaven in the form of a pure, white dove.

Her Feast is February 10th.

172

Saint Sebastian
The Soldier

Sebastian was a captain in the Roman army, a fine officer and a brave soldier.

One day he heard about Jesus Christ and said, "He is the one I want to follow." So from that day he loved Christ and fought bravely for Him.

One day his two brothers were arrested. "You are Christians, and you must die," said the judge.

They were only boys, and they were afraid. But Sebastian comforted them, saying, "Don't be afraid. We shall all be martyrs. It is glorious to die for Christ."

The Mayor of Rome did not believe in Jesus Christ. He heard about Sebastian and sent for the young soldier. "Tell me about Jesus," he ordered. And Sebastian talked so beautifully that the Mayor became a Christian too. This made the people who hated Jesus very angry. They began to kill the Christians.

Many of the Christians fled from Rome. Although Sebastian helped them escape he refused to leave.

So the Romans arrested Sebastian. They tied him to a stake. Soldiers shot at him with bows and arrows.

They left him for dead. But Sebastian was not dead. He was still alive and he went to the judge who had ordered him shot. "Please believe in Jesus," he begged. But instead they beat him to death with clubs.

His traditional Feast is January 20th.

Saint Sophia
Wisdom

Sophia lived in Italy. She was a good Christian who had three daughters named after the three Christian virtues Faith, Hope and Charity. Her husband died so she had to raise the three daughters alone. Sophia and her three daughters lived in a time when the people in charge of the government believed in other gods and wanted everyone else to believe in other gods also. They wanted to be able to control everything about the people they ruled, including their beliefs about religion. Some leaders complained about Sophia and her three daughters. They told the government that they were telling others about the love of the Lord Jesus Christ. The four were made to go to Rome and as they traveled, they prayed to the Lord to give them strength if the emperor were to torture them or even put them to death. The emperor asked them to offer sacrifice and to worship false gods, but the four of them would not go against God. The emperor had the three girls, who were only ages 12, 10 and 9, tortured in front of their mother but the girls would not go against the Faith. Sophia watched and prayed as her three daughters suffered and were finally put to death. The emperor let Sophia take her daughters to bury them and she sat beside their graves for three days. She died next to her daughters and those who were made to believe because of their Faith, came to bury her next to them. Her Feast is September 17th.

Saint Stanislaus Kostka
The Boy Saint

Stanislaus Kostka was a young Polish nobleman. His father was a rich man. So Stanislaus was brought up in the court.

Sometimes, men sitting at dinner said nasty things. When they did, little Stanislaus blushed. It made him ill to hear men say dirty and unpleasant things.

He went away to school with his big brother. But his big brother was a bully. He treated Stanislaus badly. So there was nothing to do but run away.

He did. His brother followed him with fast horses. But when they passed Stanislaus on the road, God did not let the brother see the runaway.

On that journey he came to an empty church. Oh, how he wished he could go to Holy Communion! But there was no priest. How could he receive? God took care of that. Angels brought Holy Communion to the boy. He walked all the way from Vienna to Rome.

He begged his food. The Blessed Virgin appeared to him and told him she would take care of him.

He became a Jesuit novice. From the start he showed he was a saint. He loved to pray. He was very pure.

But Mary, his Mother and ours, came for him on the Feast of the Assumption and took him with her to heaven.

His traditional Feast is November 13th.

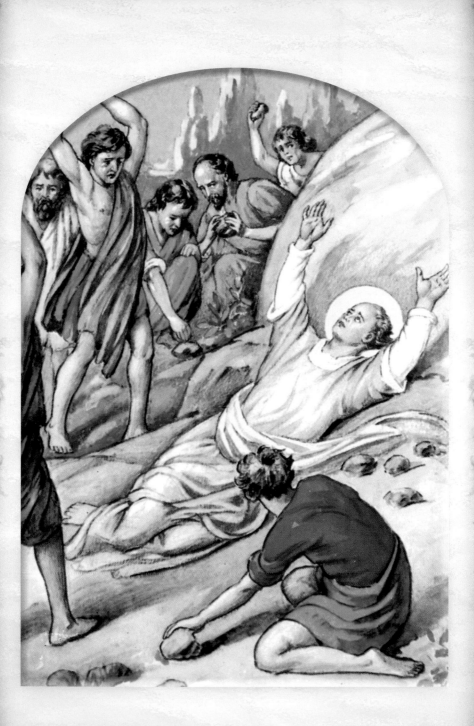

Saint Stephen
The First Martyr

Stephen loved Jesus very much. He worked hard for the poor. He told everyone that Christ was their Savior.

So many people followed him. They listened while he spoke. For his eyes were bright with love for Jesus. And he spoke beautifully of what Jesus had taught and done. One day the enemies of Jesus said, "We must stop this man. We killed Jesus. But this Stephen still makes others believe in Jesus. We must kill him too."

First they ordered him to stop preaching. He laughed. He could not stop talking about the Savior he loved. So they caught him. They dragged him outside the city.

He stood facing them, this fine young man.

He loved them because Jesus had died for their sakes. He hoped he could make them all Christians.

So he told them about Jesus. He reminded them that Jesus was the very Savior they had hoped to see. He told them that Jesus was not dead but had ascended into heaven. Angrily, they picked up rocks. They flung them at Stephen. He fell dead. But first he saw Jesus coming to take him.

He was the first martyr.

His Feast is December 26th.

Saint Teresa
The Carmelite

There were two great Saint Teresas.

One is called the Little Flower.

The other is called the Great Saint Teresa. She was the Holy Mother of the Carmelite Sisters. The Little Flower was one of her lovely spiritual children.

When the Great Teresa was a little girl, she ran away from home. Later she became a sister.

She grieved for all the sinners in the world who did not love God. "I will love Him all the harder because they do not," she said.

"Dear God," she prayed, "forgive them. See! I will suffer and do penance for their sins."

So she slept on hard boards. She never ate meat. She prayed long hours.

She said to God, "Please let me love You. Please let me suffer for their sins. And do not punish the people who hate You and who are wicked."

Many holy young women joined her.

They prayed for sinners. They asked God to keep young people from temptation. They loved God like dear daughters.

And the Great Teresa built convents for them all over the world.

They are the Carmelite Nuns.

Her Feast is October 15th.

Saint Therese
Little Flower

This little saint lived in our own times. She was a little French girl named Theresa Martin.

Even as a little girl, she wanted to belong to God alone. Since people said, "You are too young," she asked the Pope to let her be a sister. So she entered the convent when still a child.

She joined the Carmelites. She said, "I just want to love God. I want to do hard things for Him. I want to pray for priests and for sinners. I want to shine like a little candle before His altar."

Almost nobody knew about this little girl. But the minute she died, all the world seemed to hear about her. They read her story and loved her. Soldiers chose her as their patroness. She became the saint of French aviators. Priests asked her to take care of them. Catholic missions were helped with her prayers.

Before she died, she said: "After death, I will drop down from Heaven a shower of roses."

She did just that.

Theresa, the Little Flower of Jesus, has filled the world with her miracles.

Her Feast is October 1st.

Saint Thomas

Aquinas

Thomas Aquinas was a Dominican priest.

His family did not want him to be a priest. They tried very hard to stop him. But he longed to say mass and preach. In the end, he won.

Thomas became a great student. He learned to know all about Our Lord and His teachings. Young people came from all over the world to listen to his classes.

He wrote a wonderful book called the Summa.

Priests and wise men still study it today.

But he also wrote beautiful poetry and hymns. The hymns you sing at Benediction were written by Thomas.

One day Our Lord, hanging on the cross, said to Thomas: "You have written well about Me, Thomas. What reward do you wish?"

"Only yourself," answered the saint.

He knew that if he had Jesus, he had everything.

Millions of people still read the books and sing the hymns of this saint.

The Church calls him the Teacher who was like an Angel. His Feast is January 28th.

Saint Ursula

And Her Companions

When Ursula was a little girl, she loved children very much. She therefore became a teacher.

Mothers and fathers sent their boys and girls to her.

She taught them how to be good. She told them about Jesus and Mary.

She had a fine school for them in England.

But terrible pagan armies came into England. They threatened to kill all Christians. So Ursula took her pupils and her other teachers and went with them to France.

But once again, she met peril.

The terrible Huns came with their armies. They hated Jesus Christ and they killed all Christians.

So they captured Ursula and her sweet young companions.

They asked Ursula to let them make slaves of the little boys and girls. Ursula refused.

They promised to let them all go free if they would give up Christ and the Catholic faith.

They all refused.

So the army of the Huns drew their swords. They pulled back their bows and arrows. They killed Ursula and all her companions. And like glorious martyrs they went straight to heaven.

Her Feast is October 21st.

Saint Veronica
of The Way of the Cross

We only know of one important incident in the life of Saint Veronica.

This took place on the terrible day of our dear Lord's Passion. Jesus was carrying His cross. All around Him the people were laughing and screaming. They were throwing mud in His face. They were spitting upon Him. They tripped Him and made Him fall.

Jesus looked around and saw no friends. Everyone seemed to hate Him.

Then Veronica came.

She just happened to be in the crowd.

She was timid and afraid, but she wanted to help Him. So she took the veil off her head. She pushed the soldiers aside. She ran through the crowd. She came to Jesus. He had just fallen and He was too weak to stand up. Lovingly she wiped His face with her veil.

Jesus looked up gratefully. He thanked her with a smile. The soldiers pushed her away.

But when she got home and looked at her veil, she found a wonderful thing.

On the veil was a beautiful picture of Jesus. And Veronica kept that as long as she lived.

Her Feast is July 12th.

Saint Vincent
de Paul

Vincent de Paul was a very holy priest.

He remembered how Our Lord loved the poor and worked for them. So he did all he could to make life sweet and easy for them.

He gave them whatever money he had. He carried the poor sick home and took care of them in his own house. When he found poor children, he gave them food, clothing, toys, and his love.

But always he told them about Jesus Christ. He told them that the Savior was poor too, and loved the poor most of all. Once he was captured by pirates and carried away to sea.

But he made the pirate himself love Jesus Christ and became a Catholic.

To help him work for the poor, he gathered fine men and women about him. They continued his work after he died.

The men are called Priests of the Mission.

The women are the Sisters of Charity who do so much for the poor.

His traditional Feast is July 19th.

Saint William
Archbishop

William was a rich young man. He was sent to fine schools. Everyone expected him to lead an exciting, successful life.

Instead, he wanted to follow Our Lord very closely. If Jesus worked hard, he wanted to work hard too. If Jesus was poor, he preferred to be poor. Since Jesus was busy about His Father's business, young William wished this for himself.

So he became a priest when he was very young. He studied hard. He prayed well. And when he preached, people loved to listen.

But even this was not enough. He joined the poorest and hardest order of monks, called Cistercians.

He loved the prayer, peace, and quiet there. Yet the people wanted him back to care for them.

So the Pope made him Archbishop of Bourges. He did not want the honor but he obeyed the Holy Father.

William never ate meat, though he gave it to his guests and the poor. He spent no money on himself, but all on the church, the school, and the needy.

When he died, all the people followed his body to the grave, weeping.

His traditional Feast is January 10th.

Saint Zita

The Little Cook

Zita was a little cook.

She worked in the kitchen of a rich family.

They thought she was just a drudge They piled work upon her. They gave her unpleasant jobs to do.

But Zita never complained. Early in the morning, she rose and hurried off to Mass. Then she returned, got breakfast for the family, and worked all day.

"Don't work so hard,' the other servants said. "You make us ashamed of our laziness." So she did their work for them when they were tired and lazy.

One day she put the bread in the oven. Then she began to pray. She loved to talk to God. She loved to listen to Him. So she forgot her bread.

"Oh," she suddenly cried, "the bread will be burned." But it wasn't. Angels had taken it out of the oven. And no bread had ever tasted so good or smelled so sweet.

The man and woman for whom she worked grew to love her. "Teach our children to be good like you," they asked her.

So she taught their children to be saints.

She was an old, old lady when she died. And the moment she died, a bright star appeared over the room where she had slept.

Her traditional Feast is April 27th.

Contents